MW00891496

Fun with
Sizes

M
THE MILLBROOK PRESS
Brookfield, Connecticut

Published in the United States in 1998 by

M

The Millbrook Press, Inc.
2 Old New Milford Road
Brookfield, Connecticut 06804

First published in the UK in 1998 by

Belitha Press Limited
London House, Great Eastern Wharf
Parkgate Road, London SW11 4NQ

Series editor: Honor Head
Series designer: Jamie Asher
Illustrator: Kirsty Asher
U.S. Math Consultant: Henrietta Pesce

Patilla, Peter.
Fun with sizes/written by Peter Patilla; illustrated by
Kirsty Asher.
p.   cm.
Summary: Presents picture puzzles that allow the
reader to explore the concept of size.
ISBN 0-7613-0959-4 (lib. bdg.)
1. Size perception—Juvenile literature. 2. Size
judgment—Juvenile literature. 3. Picture puzzles—
Juvenile literature. [1. Size perception. 2. Picture
puzzles.] I. Asher, Kirsty, ill. II. Title.
BF299.S5P38 1998
153.7'52—dc21
98–16641
CIP AC

Printed in Hong Kong

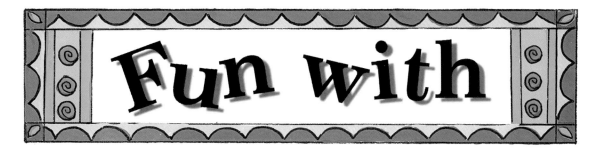

Sizes

written by
Peter Patilla

illustrated by
Kirsty Asher

About This Series

The four books in this series, *Fun With Numbers,
Fun With Shapes, Fun With Sizes,* and *Fun
With Patterns,* provide an engaging format to
explore beginning mathematical concepts with
children. They may investigate the books on
their own, but extending this investigation
with an adult will bring added value to the
experience. The following suggestions are
provided as a guide for you to help your child
or students get the most from the series.

Fun With Sizes

Size is a concept with which children interact
from a very young age. Some children enjoy
dressing up in clothing that is too big for
them, or relish the feeling of being gigantic as
they watch tiny insects. In these examples,
children are making comparisons and drawing
conclusions based on experiments with size.
Building a strong conceptual foundation with
size is necessary to later understanding in
mathematical situations. In our everyday lives
we make comparisons, evaluate situations,
and make decisions using the concept of size.

Before opening *Fun With Sizes,* talk about
the word "size." What does it mean? When is it

necessary to know the correct size? Look at the cover of the book and talk about the variety of creatures pictured. Ask children what words they would use to describe the size of a creature. Discuss why using words like big, small, long, and thin would be helpful. If a child hasn't used vocabulary that is specific to size, provide the words yourself to describe a creature. As you explore the puzzles and games in *Fun With Sizes,* use these ideas to add to the mathematical journey you are about to begin.

A Step Beyond

After you have finished exploring the book, go beyond these pages. Invite children to go on a "find the right fit" search. Gather various articles of clothing in adult and child sizes. Put everything you have gathered in a pile on the floor. Then, blindfold each child and ask them to find four items that will fit a child. Undo the blindfolds and discuss their selections. Ask, "How could you tell these shoes were the right choice? This jacket?" You will notice that the children will be using vocabulary that shows their understanding of the concept of size. Don't put the book away—children will want to open *Fun With Sizes* again and again.

The Three Bears

Match the small, medium, and big spoon, plate, honey pot, bowl, and mug to each bear.

small

medium

big

7

Long and Short

Which caterpillar is the longest?
Which spider has the shortest thread?

Wild Tracks

Find the small, medium, and big footprints...

for the lizard

for the frog

for the bird

Two of a Kind

Match the pictures below with those of the same size in the picture opposite.

13

Leap Frog

Whose jump was the longest?
Whose jump was the shortest?

Which frog has jumped the highest?

Picking Coconuts

Which ladder do you need to reach the coconuts on each tree?

17

Flower Vases

Which flowers fit in each vase?

19

Flower Chains

Which flower chain is the longest?

Which flower chains are shorter than the white one?

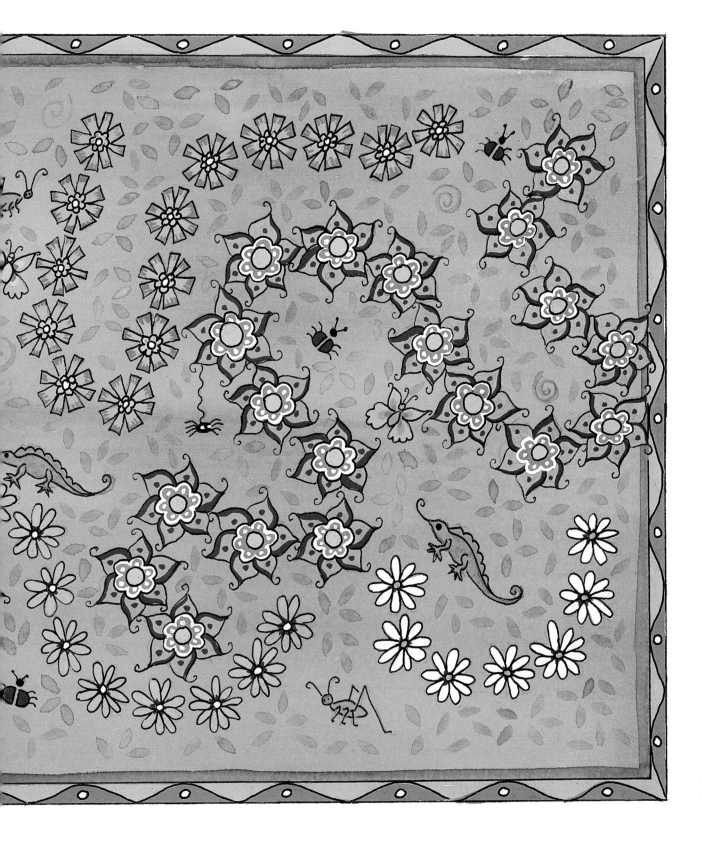

Log Cabin

Find the thinnest and the thickest log in the log cabin.

thin log   thick log

Match the logs to the trees below.

Snake Pit

Can you find the longest snake?
Can you find the shortest snake?

Fish Scales

Find the fish the same size as these.

On the Shelf

Find the tallest bottle on each shelf. Can you find the widest bottle and the smallest bottle on the shelves?

Garden of Delights

In the picture opposite can you find...

shorter flower
chains than this?

thicker vines
than this?

shorter caterpillars
than this?

taller flowers
than this?

smaller birds
than this?

Sizes

long

short

tall

thick

thin

same size

short

big

medium

small

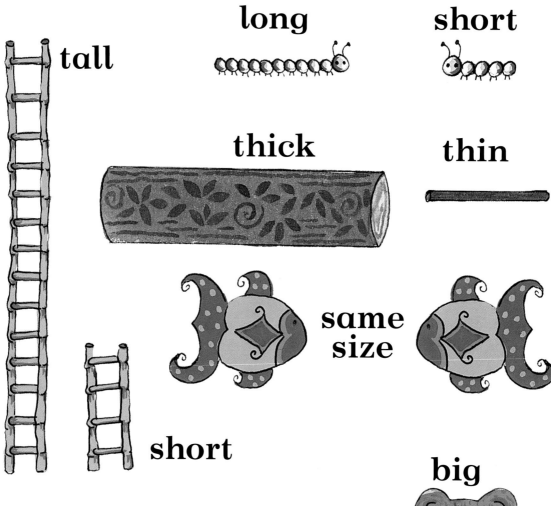